AF589264

THE SHORT VOWEL

THE ALPHABET

Practice these sounds each day until you know them well.

a apple	b banana	c cat
d dog	e egg	f flower
g glue	h horse	i igloo
j jar	k kite	l lamp
m map	n nest	o octopus
p pig	q queen	r rabbit
s sun	t toast	u umbrella
v vacuum	w water	x x-ray
y yarn	z zebra	

THE CONSONANTS

Bb	Cc	Dd
Ff	Gg	Hh
Jj	Kk	Ll
Mm	Nn	Pp
Qq	Rr	Ss
Tt	Vv	Ww
Xx	Yy	Zz

LETS REVIEW

Bb  **Ball**

Practice

ba	ba →	ll	→	ball
be	be →	ll	→	bell
bi	bi →	t	→	bit
bo	bo →	y	→	boy
bu	bu →	ll	→	bull

Read these words.

but	bit	bob
bottle	baby	been

Cc  **Car**

Practice

ca	ca →	r	→	car
ce	ce →	ll	→	cell
ci	ci →	ty	→	city
co	co →	w	→	cow
cu	cu →	p	→	cup

Read these words.

cut	cat	circle
celery	coat	cook

Dd Dawn

Practice

da	da → wn → dawn
de	de → n → den
di	di → p → dip
do	do → g → dog
du	du → ck → duck

Read these words.

did	dan	dark
dust	doll	desk

Ff  **Fast**

Practice

fa	fa → st → fast
fe	fe → d → fed
fi	fi → ll → fill
fo	fo → x → fox
fu	fu → n → fun

Read these words.

fit	fud	fur
fact	fell	fox

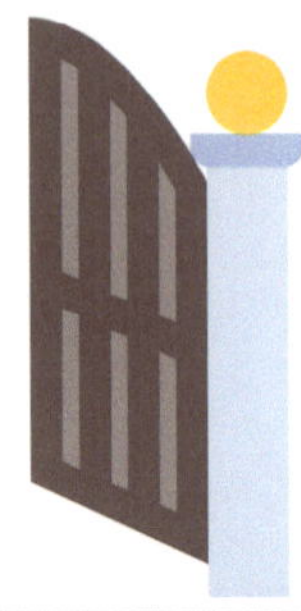

Gate

Practice

ga	ga	te	→	gate
ge	ge	l	→	gel
gi	gi	rl	→	girl
go	go	ne	→	gone
gu	gu	y	→	guy

Read these words.

gap	gone	gem
guide	gum	girl

Hh  Hat

Practice

ha ha → t → hat

he he → n → hen

hi hi → t → hit

ho ho → p → hop

hu hu → t → hut

Read these words.

hope	hunt	hay
heart	hatch	hide

Jj  **Jar**

Practice

ja	ja → r	→ jar
je	je → t	→ jet
ji	ji → g	→ jig
jo	jo → y	→ joy
ju	ju → g	→ jug

Read these words.

jet	jinx	jog
jake	jump	jolly

Kk  **kale**

Practice

ka	ka	→	le	→	kale
ke	ke	→	n	→	ken
ki	ki	→	te	→	kite
ko	ko	→	t	→	kot
ku	ku	→	dos	→	kudos

Read these words.

ken	kudos	kot
karma	kick	king

Ll  lamp

Practice

la	la → mp → lamp
le	le → d → led
li	li → ve → live
lo	lo → g → log
lu	lu → ng → lung

Read these words.

lot	lung	leg
last	laugh	lip

Mm 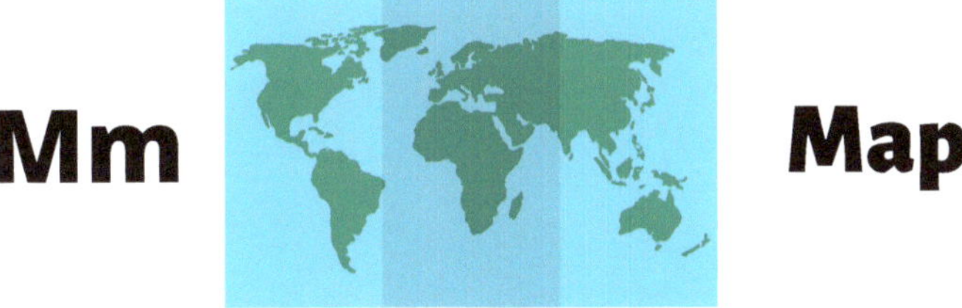 **Map**

Practice

ma	ma	→	p	→	map
me	me	→	t	→	met
mi	mi	→	ll	→	mill
mo	mo	→	m	→	mom
mu	mu	→	g	→	mug

Read these words.

mud	men	may
mat	mix	mop

Nn  **Nap**

Practice

na	na	→ p	→	nap
ne	ne	→ t	→	net
ni	ni	→ t	→	nit
no	no	→ b	→	nob
nu	nu	→ t	→	nut

Read these words.

nap	nine	nut
ned	none	note

Pp  **Paw**

Practice

pa	pa → w	→	paw
pe	pe → t	→	pet
pi	pi → n	→	pin
po	po → t	→	pot
pu	pu → t	→	put

Read these words.

pat	peter	put
pitch	pond	pay

Qq  **Quake**

Practice

Qua	qua → ke →	quake
Que	que → en →	queen
Qui	qui → ck →	quick
Quo	quo → te →	quote
Qu	qu → iz →	quiz

Read these words.

Quiz Queen Quit
Quote Quake

Rr 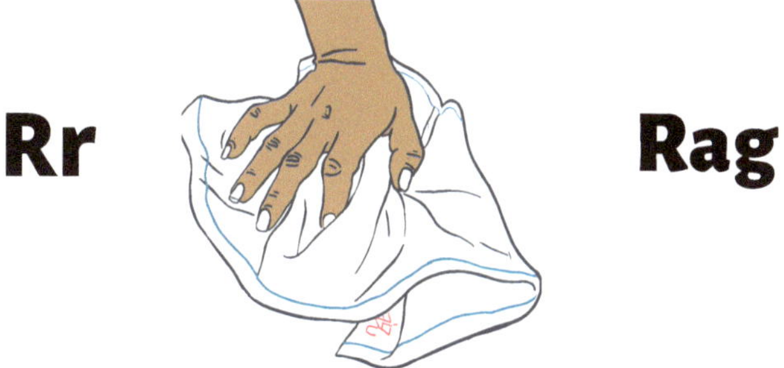 **Rag**

Practice

ra	ra → g	→	rag
re	re → d	→	red
ri	ri → p	→	rip
ro	ro → t	→	rot
ru	ru → n	→	run

Read these words.

rat	rib	rug
red	rock	rod

Ss  **Sad**

Practice

sa	sa → d	→	sad
se	se → t	→	set
si	si → p	→	sip
so	so → n	→	son
su	su → n	→	sun

Read these words.

sum	six	sand
sun	soap	set

Practice

ta	ta → g → tag
te	te → n → ten
ti	ti → p → tip
to	to → p → top
tu	tu → b → tub

Read these words.

toy	tub	tow
tan	ten	tin

Vv  **Van**

Practice

va	va	→	n	→	van
ve	ve	→	t	→	vet
vi	vi	→	ne	→	vine
vo	vo	→	w	→	vow
vu	vu	→	m	→	vum

Read these words.

void	vum	vine
very	violin	vase

walk

Practice

wa wa → lk → walk

we we → t → wet

wi wi → nk → wink

wo wo → w → wow

wu wu → d → wud

Read these words.

water	wud	woke
worry	west	wing

Xx  **wax**

Practice

a	wa	→	x	→	wax
e	re	→	flex	→	reflex
i	fi	→	x	→	fix
o	bo	→	x	→	box
u	tu	→	x	→	tux

Read these words.

wax	box	tux
fix	reflex	tax

Yy 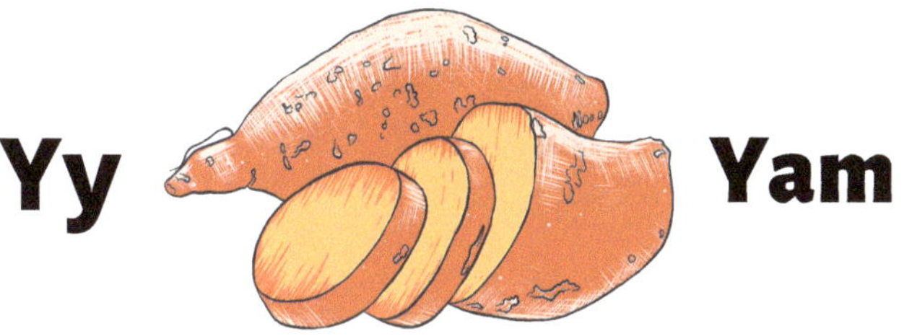 **Yam**

Practice

ya	ya	→	m	→	yam
ye	ye	→	ll	→	yell
yi	yi	→	eld	→	yield
yo	yo	→	u	→	you
yu	yu	→	m	→	yum

Read these words.

yum	yam	yes
young	yell	yikes

Zz  **Zap**

Practice

za za → p → zap

ze ze → bra → zebra

zi zi → pper → zipper

zo zo → om → zoom

zu zu → cchini → zucchini

Read these words.

zap	zoom	zebra
zag	zipper	zucchini

THE LONG VOWEL

REVIEW THE LONG VOWEL

bead
read
cheat
meat

need
feed
jeep
keep
beep

dime
time
lime

book
look
boot
hoop

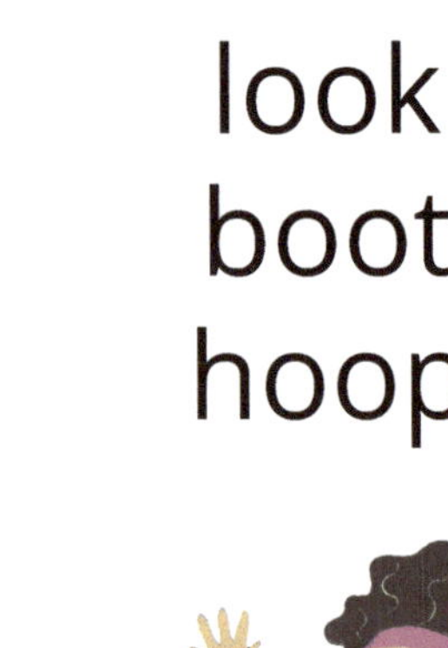

vote
joke
pole

music
mule

boat
coat

LETS REVIEW

SHORT VOWELS	LONG VOWELS
Aa	Aa
Ee	Ee
Ii	Ii
Oo	Oo
Uu	Uu

LEARNING SIGHT WORDS

Sight word: a

Mom made Jake a cake.

Sight word: to

We like to go fast.

Sight word: I

I like the cho co la te.

Sight word: is

Corey is a part of the team.

Sight word: do

I do activities with mom

Sight word: are

Joy and Troy are twins.

Sight word: the

I see the school bus.

Sight word: for

They ran for a long time.

Sight word: has

she has the same socks.

Sight word: did

Chris did great .

SPECIAL SOUNDS

1.tra tre tri tro tru

train tree trip troop trust

---

sh **shell**

2.sha she shi sho shu

shape shell ship shop shut

SPECIAL SOUNDS

th **throw**

3.tha the thi tho thu

that them thick throw thumb

---

st **star**

4.sta ste sti sto stu

star step stick stop stuck

SPECIAL SOUNDS

ck  **duck**

5.ack eck ick ock uck

sack neck pick knock duck

ay  **hay**

6.ay

hay play lay stay way

SPECIAL SOUNDS

est **tallest**

7. est

tallest thickest cutest
deepest honest

---

ly **brightly**

8.ly

gladly brightly quickly
certainly softly

PREFIX

en **enjoy**

1. enlarge
2. enjoy
3. engage
4. enable
5. endure

PREFIX

un **untidy**

1. untidy
2. unhappy
3. unfold
4. unbutton
5. undo

SUFFIX

1. jumping
2. playing
3. sitting
4. running
5. painting

jogging
learning
flying
eating
morning

SUFFIX

1. toasted
2. packed
3. fished
4. cooked
5. snowed

painted

counted

needed

shouted

walked

PRACTICE SPECIAL SOUNDS

Special sound: tr

E'lijah wants to ride the train.

He will take a trip.

Special sound: ck

Demi wants to pick berries.

She will put them in a sack.

PRACTICE PREFIX AND SUFFIX

Prefix: un

Tom always seems unhappy.
His room is untidy.

Suffix: ing

Khi'von loves eating pancakes.

He eats pancakes every morning.

You did it!

Remember to Read all sounds as often as possible!
Practice
Practice
Practice
Makes for a great beginner reader!

www.ingramcontent.com/pod-product-compliance
Ingram Content Group UK Ltd.
Pitfield, Milton Keynes, MK11 3LW, UK
UKHW061024310726
14090UKWH00023B/77

* 9 7 9 8 5 0 2 3 2 0 7 7 1 *